The Story of Aum

written and conceived by
Maria C. Hamburger
watercolor paintings and graphic design by
Patricia P. Kay

The Story of Aum

ISBN **0-9759226-1-0**

Illustration: Patricia P. Kay
Design and production: Steve Carroll

Steve Carroll Printing/Brain Friendly Learning
6801 6th Street, NW
Washington, DC 20012
202-723-7337
stevecarroll@speakeasy.net

Library of Congress Cataloging-in-Publication Data
Hamburger, Maria C., 1963-
The Story of Aum

The symbol of Aum

represents God, love and all of creation.
Though we may live in many different places
with various cultures and religions,
Aum reminds us that we are all connected.

Aum is the love in your heart and mine.

(Can you find the symbol of Aum in each picture?)

Dedicated to Andy, Alex, and Oliver
who have taught me the fullness of love ,
and
to my teacher Suzie Hurley who has shown me the journey to the heart.

Maria C. Hamburger

In the vacuum of nothingness
and silence
Where space only filled space

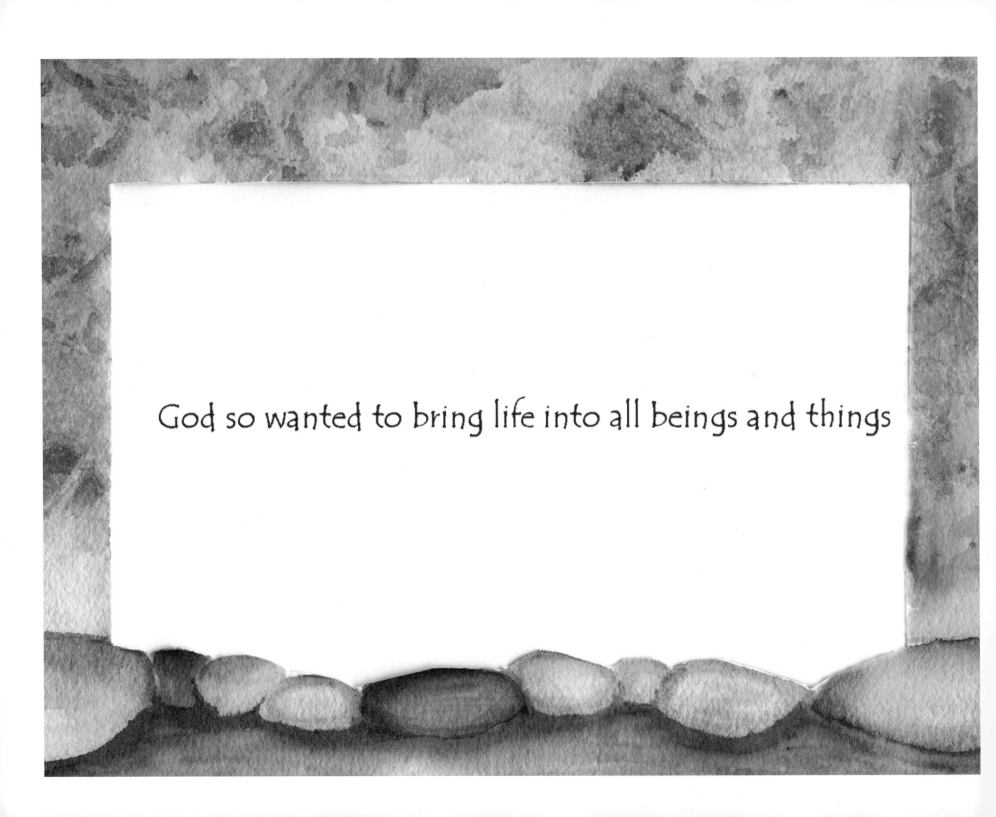

God so wanted to bring life into all beings and things

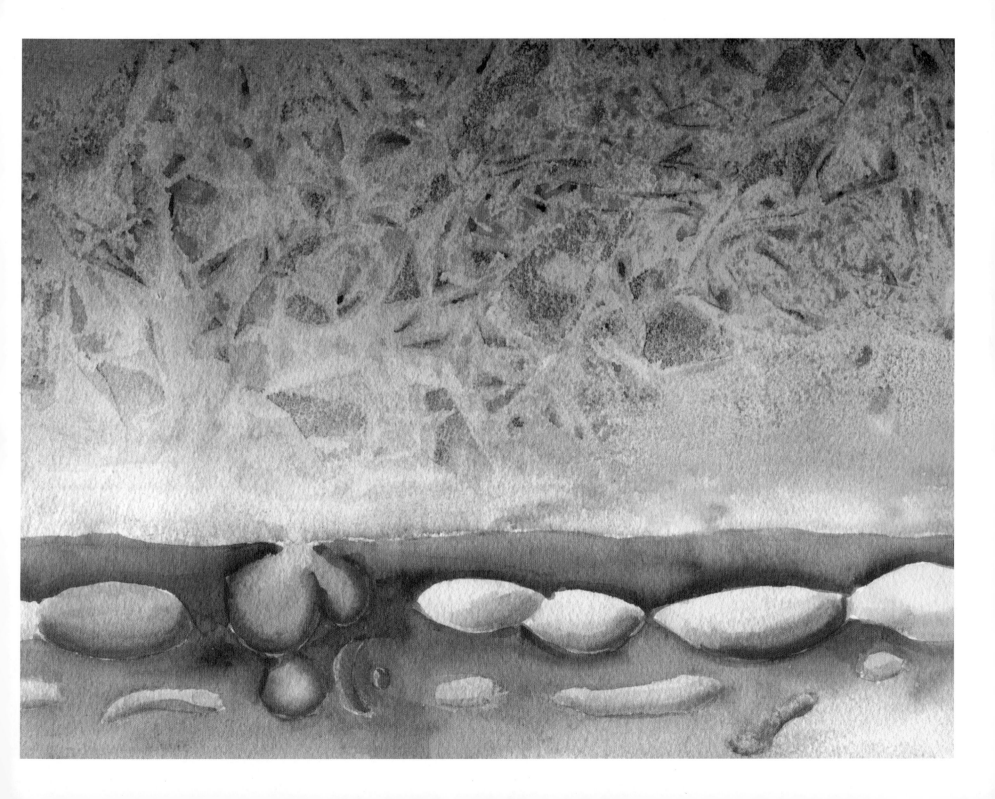

There stirred up the most powerful vibration
Awakening the sleeping nothingness all around

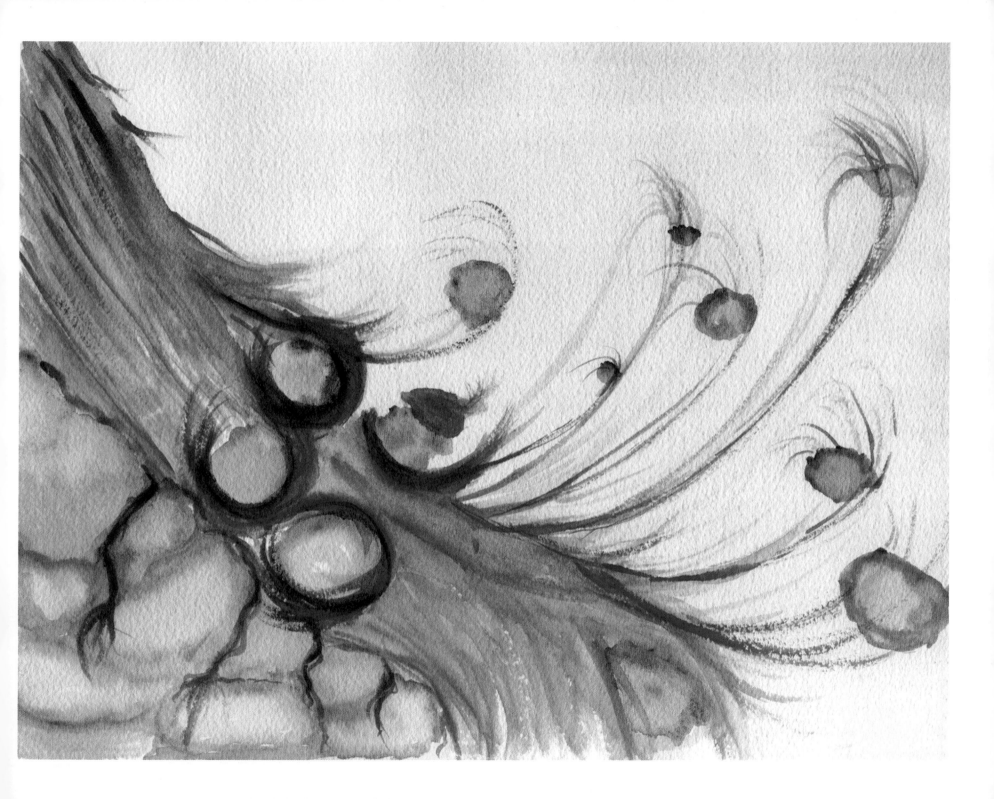

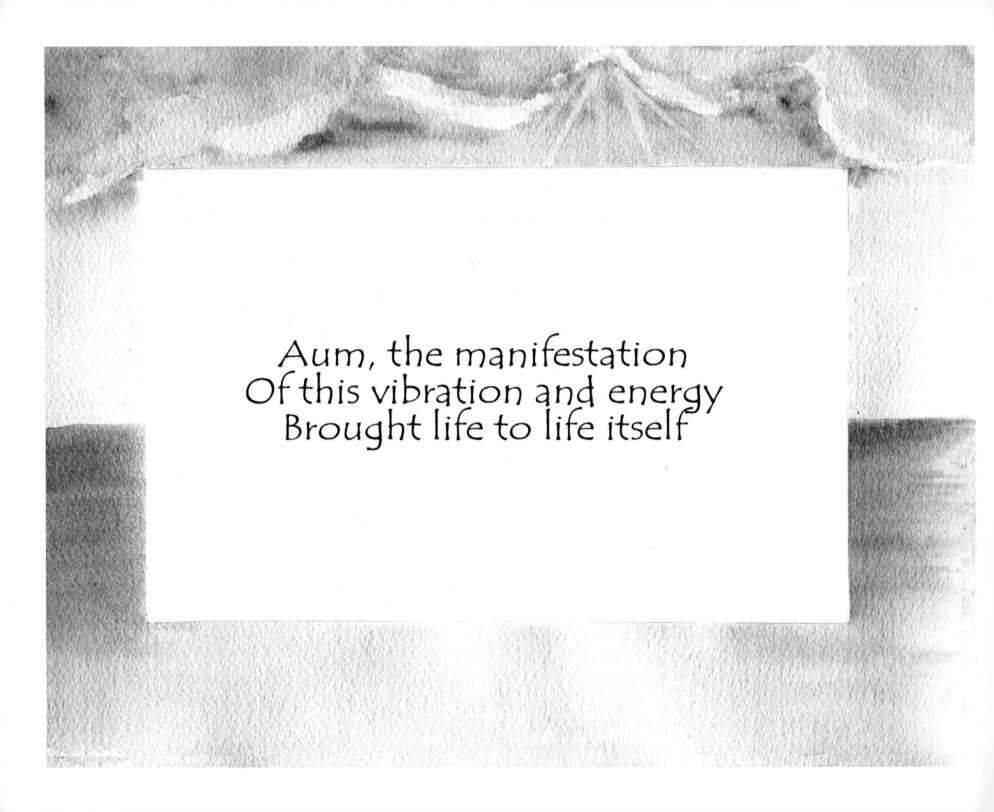

Aum, the manifestation
Of this vibration and energy
Brought life to life itself

Days became days, nights became nights,
Mountains, trees, stars and you and me BECAME !

Thunder roared and oceans filled with water
Animals roamed the land

Life began in all creatures large and small

Aum gave birth to words
So that we could give meanings and names
To all beings and things and thoughts
Love and sadness, joy and life

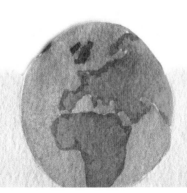
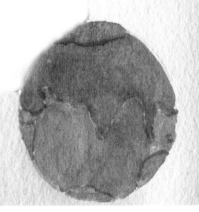

God's first intention was love

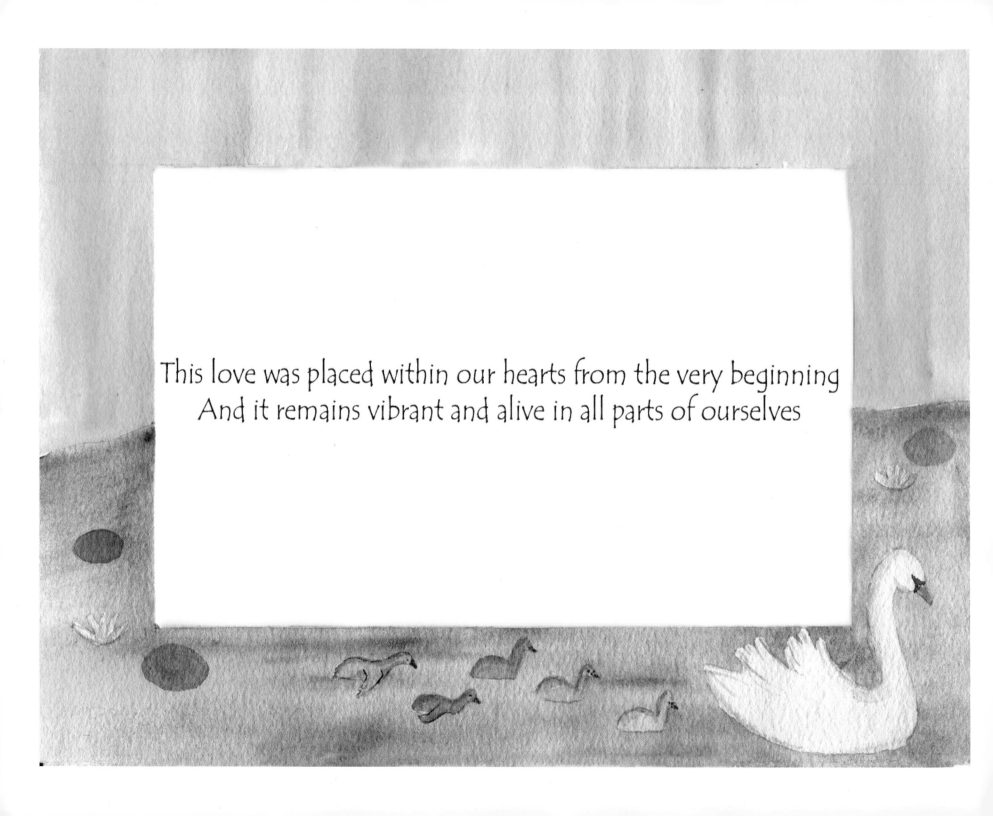

This love was placed within our hearts from the very beginning
And it remains vibrant and alive in all parts of ourselves

It is the fiber that weaves through all parts of ourselves
Our bodies, our minds, thoughts, feelings and hearts
Vibrating in all beings
As the thread that connects us to one another

Aum is the presence of God and love
In each and every one of us

AUM

AUM

Going back approximately 6000 years to Vedic times the sacred syllable AUM expresses the pulse
of the Universe itself. It represents our connection with the universe from the beginning of
creation to our present and future world.

Each geometric curve on the symbol of AUM represents a different state of consciousness: waking,
sleeping and dreaming, and the fourth state of consciousness, the transcendent or Turya
which underlies and supports the other three.

AUM is also an essential part of the spiritual practice of yoga. When chanted, the vibrations of
the letters themselves, A-U-M, travel from the back to the front of the mouth, recalling the
different states of consciousness. The sound of AUM is said to have been the first sound, the
first Word, from which all creation emerged.

AUM resonates in our present world as the essence of the Divine in all beings, unifying us to each
other and to the universe.

Aum gave birth to words - a guide to meanings

Word (Greek)

Woman (Chinese)

Peace (Hebrew)

Aum (Sanskrit)

God (Swahili)

Love (Serbian)

Life (Korean)

Peace (Chinese)

Birth (Persian)

Son (Russian)

Home (Japanese)

God (Sanskrit)

God (Arabic)

Life (Ancient Egyptian heiroglyphics)

I Love You (American sign Language)

Love (Latin)

Peace (French)